ATONEMENT FOR WHOM?

A STUDY OF THE HIGH PRIESTHOOD OF JESUS CHRIST

"For he hath made him to be sin for us, who knew no sin; that we might be made the righteousness of God in him." {II Cor.5:21}

Moreno Dal Bello

ATONEMENT FOR WHOM?

A STUDY OF THE HIGH PRIESTHOOD OF JESUS CHRIST

Most people who have been brought up attending churches for all, or most, of their lives and even those who are newcomers to 'churchianity' are seldom, if ever, encouraged to study the high-priesthood of the Old Testament which was a shadow or type of the true High Priesthood of the Messiah Who was to come—Jesus Christ. Most are subtly conditioned by their religious leaders to leave such *'high theological issues'* to their *'pastors'* and other such intellects who are *'best equipped to handle such intricate matters of religious study'.* But to learn about God and to know Who He is and what He has done is not, and never has been, the prerogative for the intellectual elite among us but it should be, and is, what the heart of the true seeker of God yearns for—**to know the true God and to know what He has done.** Jesus Christ has stated: ***"And this is life eternal, THAT THEY MIGHT KNOW THEE the only true God, and Jesus Christ, Whom Thou hast sent"*** (Jn. 17:3). **Before one can know, and therefore believe in the True God, one must hear His True Gospel wherein the Righteousness of His Son Jesus Christ is revealed** (Rom. 1:16,17).

The Gospel of God teaches that man is dead in sin (Rom. 5:12) and cannot in and of himself come to the True God in the way that God has prescribed (Rom. 3:10-12). Therefore it is God Who must come to man, purely by Sovereign grace, if any man is to be saved (Titus 3:7). Jesus the Lord told His disciples that with man salvation is impossible but that with God all things are possible, even the salvation of a man (Matt. 19:26). Man's best efforts at obedience gain nothing for him with God. Scripture says, ***"...verily every man at his best state is altogether vanity"*** (Psa. 39:5), and ***"..we are all as an unclean thing, and all our righteousnesses are as filthy rags..."***

(Isa. 64:6; see also Job 15:16). This coincides with the Scripture found in Ephesians 2:12 which tells us that **a man without God is without hope in this world.** So, then, man is elected to salvation by the Sovereign God purely by grace and not according to anything that man has done. The Bible states clearly: **"Not by works of righteousness which we have done, but according to His mercy He saved us..."** (Titus 3:5; see also 2 Tim. 1:9). All whom God has appointed to salvation **will**, at the predetermined time, come to Him for He has decreed it (see Acts 13:48 & Jn. 6:37). These ones will receive eternal life and shall never perish (Jn. 10:27,28; Rom. 11:29). The requirements of the law of God for perfect righteousness are fulfilled by the righteousness of Christ being imputed to all those whom the Lord had given Him (Rom. 4:6). **But what of their sins?** This booklet will show conclusively that the Lord Jesus Christ was appointed, in His role as Savior and High Priest, the Representative of **not every individual in the whole world, but exclusively for those whom God the Father had elected to eternal life.** The very role or office, as we shall see, of the high priest alone, bears this out.

To understand the office of the high priest we need to turn to the Old Testament, for therein we shall find the first mention of a priesthood chosen by God to fulfill all that He had planned, **not for the whole world**, but for His people alone who at that time, and in a temporal sense, was the nation of Israel. Understanding the role of the high priest in the Old Testament is vital to a proper and biblical understanding of the New Testament atonement for sin— **how it was accomplished and for whom it was performed**—because the high priest of the Old Testament was merely a *type* or *shadow* of the True Great High Priest, Jesus Christ the Son of God, Who would come. *"A type is something emblematic or symbolic, used to express, embody, represent or forecast, some person, truth or event. It is an image or similitude of something else, sustaining to doctrinal teaching some such relation as a picture does to a precept or promise, representing to the eye or imagination a concept addressed to the ear or understanding. It is one of the most frequent forms of figurative teaching in Scripture..."*

(A.T. Pearson). *"The Old Testament types were a mode of instruction of the way in which God was to be approached..."* A type is also a prophetic symbol. *"God has graciously adapted a series of types, historical and ceremonial, to the illustration of His wondrous plan* (of redemption as revealed in the Gospel), *and especially to portray the various aspects of the office and work of Christ...By the typical system, God was not only educating His people for the 'good things to come,' but was also preparing human language to be a fit medium for the revelation of His grace in Christ. It is to the types we must turn if we would define aright the sacrificial terms of the New Testament....the doctrinal statements of the Epistles are frequently couched in the language of the types, and can only be rightly interpreted in the light which they furnish"* (A.W. Pink). It is true that Christ died, but the Word of God states one vital aspect of His death and that is **"...that Christ died for our sins ACCORDING TO THE SCRIPTURES"** (1 Cor. 15:3). This not only means that Christ died according to Old Testament prophecies but that He would die according to the Old Testament types which foreshadowed His Sacrifice and pointed to His High Priesthood. One needs to keep in mind what the New Testament says about the Old Testament: **"For whatsoever things were written aforetime were written for our learning, that we through patience and comfort of the Scriptures might have hope"** (Rom. 15:4).

What the Old Testament high priest did for God's people in a temporal sense, Jesus Christ the Great High Priest did for God's people in an eternal sense. **The Old Testament high priest did what he did for the people of God from one nation, Israel. Jesus Christ as High Priest did what He did for God's chosen people from among EVERY nation.** To be a child of God has never been conditioned on a man's choice of God but on God's choosing man—on His election of man. Christ was the Substance, the fulfillment of all that the Old Testament high priest purposed to do under the directive of God , but could never do eternally for those whom God had chosen. The fact that the blood of the sacrifices offered up by the Old Testament high priest could never take away sins, showed that this was a type of what the true High Priest Who was to come who would offer up, His own blood, which alone could take away sins eternally. Otherwise there would have been no need for Christ to come and offer up His own blood (Heb. 7:11). **"And every priest standeth daily ministering and offering oftentimes the same sacrifices, which can never take away sins: But this man (Jesus Christ), after he had offered ONE sacrifice for sins FOREVER, sat down on the right hand of God"** (Heb. 10:11,12). To understand this, to have this clear in one's mind and heart, is to gain a proper understanding of what atonement is, who atonement was made for and releases a person from a state of darkness when it comes to the Gospel, showing them precisely what the Gospel is all about, what atonement and redemption are and who it has been performed and obtained for.

Leviticus 16:16,17 is where we find just who the high priest was directed by God to make atonement for: **"And he (the high priest) shall make an atonement for the holy place, because of the uncleanness of the children of Israel, and because of their transgressions in all their sins: and so shall he do for the tabernacle of the congregation, that remaineth among them in the midst of their uncleanness. And there shall be no man in the tabernacle of the congregation when he goeth in to make an atonement in the holy place, until he come out, and have made an atonement for himself, and for his household, and for ALL THE CONGREGATION OF ISRAEL." It is vital to a proper understanding of what atonement is, to notice who atonement was made for in the Old Testament, whilst being mindful of the fact that this was a blueprint of what would happen in the New Testament.** Atonement was made exclusively for the nation of Israel and no other. **Atonement was made, not for those who would end up choosing God, but atonement was made on the behalf of the people whom God had ALREADY chosen.** In none of the various *typical* sacrifices, as set out by God, were any other people determined by God to reap the benefits but that one small nation, Israel. It must be understood from the outset, and it is vital that a person be convinced, that **the Old Testament**

high priest was directed by the Lord God to make an atonement, not for the sins of every individual in the entire world, but for one nation and one nation only— Israel, who were at that time, and on a temporary basis, the people of God. So, too, Jesus Christ as High Priest made atonement for spiritual Israel—the eternal people of God—the true seed of Abraham (Rom. 9:6-8; see also Isa. 53:10). The people of Israel were the sole beneficiaries of the atonement for sin made by the high priest in the Old Testament, for they were a chosen nation, and at that time, the people of God. **No atonement was ever made for the peoples of other nations.** The physical nation of Israel was never chosen to be the eternal people of God. This is evident in verses such as Romans 9:6: **"...they which are the children of the flesh, these are NOT the children of God: but the children of the PROMISE are counted for the seed."** This means that the people who were the physical descendants of Abraham were not the true Israel of God. The true Israel of God, spiritual Israel, is made up of those who have had their hearts circumcised (Phil. 3:3), those who are the spiritual descendants of Abraham **"And if ye be Christ's, then are ye Abraham's seed, and heirs according to the promise"** (Gal 3:29). The people of the physical nation of Israel received temporal blessings. They received the exclusive attention of God, but on a temporary basis. The covenant which God had made with the nation of Israel was not an eternal one, but rather a temporal one for the express purposes God had designed it for (Heb. 8:6-10). The animal sacrifices were not to continue forever, for they pointed to the One Great and True sacrifice, that of Jesus Christ (Heb. 10:8-10).

Most people today are taught that Christ Jesus died for every single individual ever born. Sadly, this teaching may be found just as surely in a Protestant assembly as in a gathering of Roman Catholics. Teachings such as these, primarily show an incredible amount of ignorance of what the True Gospel is and show a distinct lack of understanding by those who profess to be believers in churches today which claim to be preaching salvation, about atonement—what it is and who it was made for. **What people are being taught** about Jesus Christ and His atoning death upon the cross is a lie. The gravity of the situation cannot be emphasized too highly.** To deny or to be ignorant of what Christ has done, is to deny Christ Himself. The True Redemptive Character of God and the True Atoning work of Christ have been, and continue to be, grossly misrepresented in churches today. **They are not preaching God's Gospel, but a counterfeit in which there is no salvation.** It is hoped that this booklet will make it clear to all who read it exactly what biblical atonement is and for whom it was made. It is not necessary, in achieving this goal, to launch into some exhaustive study of the details of **what** the high priest in the Old Testament actually did in order to successfully perform his duties, as ordered by God, so as to make proper atonement on behalf of those he represented. The main aim of this booklet is to show from Scripture for **WHOM** it was that the Lord Jesus Christ, acting as the Great High Priest, the only One who could make full atonement for all the sins His precious blood was shed, actually made atonement. A correct biblical understanding of exactly who Christ Jesus has made atonement for is an extremely serious issue, for it reveals whether a person has been taught of God or not. It is not an incidental teaching which does not have any relevance to a person's being saved or not, but has everything to do with a person knowing the true Gospel of Jesus Christ. Those who think that precisely what Christ did on the cross is just some theological sticking point among fellow 'believers' have got it drastically wrong. **Who one believes Christ has died for reveals exactly what that person believes Jesus did on the cross.** Far from being just a matter of high theology which can be debated amongst 'brethren' this is the core of Christianity itself. **Who Christ is and what Christ has done is revealed in the Gospel by who Jesus died for on the cross.** If one believes that Christ has died for every individual, then one holds to a salvation conditioned on the sinner's choice to accept or reject what has been done. If one holds to what the Bible teaches, that Christ died for His people, the elect of God, then one holds to the truth that what Christ did was actually obtain redemption for them by His death (Heb. 9:12). This is not a side issue to be studied on a religious whim but is an essential to salvation. Ignorance of God's Gospel is evidence of lostness: **"But if our Gospel be hid, it is hid to them that are lost"** (2 Cor. 4:3).

The subject of the high priesthood and atonement is really a very simple one to deal with, when one knows what the Gospel of God is all about. One can only trust in the true Christ AFTER one has heard the True Gospel (Eph. 2:13; see also Rom.10:17). **A Christian is not one who decides to believe in God and then learns about Him—Who He is and what He has done, a Christian is a person who has heard of God as He is revealed in the Gospel and is then given the faith, by grace, to believe that Gospel.** As was mentioned earlier, the state of every man, by nature, is that he is dead in his sin by means of the Fall in the Garden of Eden: **"Wherefore, as by one man sin entered into the world, and death by sin; and so death passed upon all men, for that all have sinned"** (Rom. 5:12). God had told Adam that in the day he ate of the fruit of the tree of the knowledge of good and evil **HE WOULD SURELY DIE** (Gen. 2:16,17). This meant that not only would the curse of physical death be introduced to the entire race of man by way of Adam's sin, but that even more seriously Adam and his race would die SPIRITUALLY, that is, they would all be eternally separated from God because of Adam's sin—his decision to disobey God and follow the lie of Satan which was that Adam would not die if he ate of the forbidden fruit (Gen. 3:4) and that this disobedience would be beneficial to Adam. This is seen in Adams not dying physically in the moment he ate of the fruit. Man in this dreadful and deplorable state of lostness was, the Bible says, now **WITHOUT HOPE** BECAUSE HE WAS **WITHOUT GOD** IN THIS WORLD! (Eph.2:12). Few people ever really understand fully the deadly implications of the terrible fact about the lost condition every man is in from birth. Man is a product of sin. **Man is born a child of the Devil and must be born AGAIN (spiritually) to become a child of God.** Sin begets sin and sinners beget sinners. Just like a dog cannot but give birth to another dog, so too, sinful man cannot but give birth to his own kind. **It is important to note that all who believe man is merely sin-sick, believe and promote Satan's lie to Eve that**

she would not surely die, for they say "we are not surely dead". One cannot believe and teach the true Gospel if one holds to such a lie.

If man, without God, has no hope of salvation, then it stands to biblical reason that with God, and only with God, he does have hope. But it must be stated quite emphatically **that it is not because God enables a man to do something that will please God, which makes a man acceptable to a Holy God.** Not at all. That is not what the grace of God is all about. God's **grace** is what saves a man: **"...being justified by His grace..."** (Titus 3:7). It is true that salvation is by grace **through** faith, but that faith is not a work of man's but a gift from God: **"For by grace are ye saved through faith; and that not of yourselves: it is the gift of God: Not of works, lest any man should boast"** (Eph. 2:8,9). Salvation by grace is not about God's enabling a man to do anything in order to merit salvation, for then salvation would be by a mixture of God's favor and man's works. This cannot be so for Paul the apostle has said: **"Even so then at this present time also there is a remnant according to the ELECTION OF GRACE. And if by grace, then is it no more of works: otherwise grace is no more grace. But if it be of works, THEN IS IT NO MORE OF GRACE: otherwise work is no more work"** (Rom. 11:5,6). Paul is saying here that if election is by the grace of God, then it cannot be by a man's efforts. Paul himself counted all the religious duties he had performed, before being saved, as dung: **"Yea doubtless, and I count all things but loss for the excellency of the knowledge of Christ Jesus my Lord: for Whom I have suffered the loss of all things, and do count them but dung, that I may win Christ, and be found in Him not having mine own righteousness, which is of the law (works), but that which is through the faith of Christ, the righteousness which is of God by faith"** (Phil 3:8,9). God has reserved for Himself (Rom. 11:4)–elected–a people according to His grace and not according to man's works. What Romans 11:6 is saying is that election unto salvation is solely according to God's grace and not man's works. **If it was according to man's works in any way, to any**

degree, then salvation would no longer be of grace. Grace and works are like oil and water, **the two cannot be mixed.** Salvation is purely by the grace, the effort, the work of a Sovereign God Who does whatsoever He wills and Who saves whomsoever He wills (Jn. 17:2 & Isa. 46:10). Salvation is a gift which cannot be merited by sinful man. Just as a house key cannot open a car door, so too, salvation cannot be obtained by a man's works, which is why it comes to a man as a gift from God **solely by grace.** Salvation is so precious and glorious a thing that it is quite unattainable by man. This is why salvation is a gift of God and not something which is merited by a work of man's, **with or without God's help.** It is not by the works which a man can do, the Bible says, lest any man should boast (Eph. 2:8,9). It is not something which man has achieved and can therefore vaunt, but something which he has been given and can only be thankful for.

This established, we understand that salvation is a free gift given by a Sovereign God, according to His grace, to a people of **His** own choosing who have done nothing to merit it. The very fact that the grace of God is something which man can do nothing to acquire, is proof positive that it is God Who chooses the recipients of it. **Salvation is given to a people whom God has chosen to reserve unto Himself.** The nation of Israel in the Old Testament was not chosen by God because of any merit that nation had gained with God for the nation itself did not even exist. God had chosen to make of Abraham one nation whom God would call His people. God has elected a people from every nation on earth to become His very own people—a people peculiar to God **"and hast redeemed us to God by Thy blood out of every kindred, and tongue, and people, and nation"** (Rev. 5:9). We must mention that all whom God has elected or chosen or reserved unto Himself or wants to save, WILL UNDOUBTEDLY BE SAVED, for God does whatsoever He wants and whatsoever He wants He does (Eph. 1:11). God does not fail. God does not wish or hope for something only to see it never come to pass. God is not like us. God is God and He gets all He wants. His every desire and thought is fulfilled to the letter. If it were otherwise He would not be

God: **"And all the inhabitants of the earth are reputed as nothing: and He doeth according to His will in the army of heaven, and among the inhabitants of the earth: and none can stay His hand, or say unto Him, What doest Thou?"** (Dan. 4:35). Biblical reasoning would then demand that all whom God has elected to salvation, will not only be saved, but will be **eternally** saved. A saved man is made alive to God **by God,** and that eternally. **True Life is not merely living eternally but being made eternally alive to God.** The salvation which comes from God is an eternal salvation and not a temporary one. God's people **"...have passed from death unto life..."** (1 Jn. 3:14). They have been saved from sin and that eternally. The life which a saved man has been given is ETERNAL Life: **"...the gift of God is eternal life through Jesus Christ our Lord"** (Rom.6:23). Therefore they have been saved unto God, and for God, forever.

But God electing a people was not enough in order to secure their salvation. God's law and justice had to be satisfied or else there would be no salvation. God is a Just God and what He does must be in perfect conformity with His Holy Character, or He would cease to be God. God is Love, but *"God does not sacrifice His Holiness to His love."* God does not *do* what is right; whatever God does **IS** right. God's Holy Law must be fulfilled perfectly if any one is to have the righteousness which God's law demands a man must be clothed with, in order to enter heaven. As we have shown, the Bible clearly teaches that man cannot attain righteousness, or right standing with God, by works of the law, that is by his attempts at obeying God's law, for man in his sinful hopeless condition can never obey God's law perfectly: **"...by the works of the law shall no flesh be justified"** (Gal. 2:16) and **"...all have sinned, and come short of the glory of God"** (Rom. 3:23). Therefore, if a man is to have the righteousness which God's law demands, it must be given to him as a gift. Man must be clothed with a covering acceptable to a Holy God. This was evidenced immediately after the Fall. *"In the Divine clothing of our first parents with* **"coats of skins"** *(Gen. 3:21), there were illustrated the facts that: fallen man needed an external* *covering to fit him to stand before God; that he could not produce this by his own labors; that the life of an innocent victim must be taken, in order to provide a suitable covering for him; that God Himself must provide it. In the offering of Abel and God's acceptance of the same (Gen. 4:4), we learn that God can only regard any sinner with favor by virtue of his acceptance in Christ"* (A.W. Pink). This requirement has been fulfilled by the Lord Jesus Christ who lived a perfect life and obeyed God faultlessly, even to dying on a cross, not for Himself but for the people whom God had given Him. All those whom God has elected unto salvation have/will be clothed with the perfect Righteousness which God's law demands. Christ's Righteousness is imputed, or charged, to them (Rom. 4:6).

This leaves us with one remaining issue: **the sins of those very people whom God has elected.** They could never, in and of themselves, make up for their sins, for in everything a person does he sins again. Even the love for God which a child of God has, falls way short of how we should love Him, for we do not love Him perfectly. Man could do nothing about his sin problem, so again God would be the one required to do something. **And do something He has!!** God sent His only Son to this earth to live a perfect life of obedience to God's law and to die on a cross for the sins of God's people. Just as the children of God were to have His perfect Righteousness imputed unto them, Christ Jesus has had their sins imputed unto Him: **"For He hath made Him to be sin for us, Who knew no sin; that we might be made the righteousness of God in Him"** (2 Cor. 5:21). This is known as Imputation—the Just dying for the unjust (1 Pet. 3:18). *"The substitution of Christ in the sinner's place was most distinctly shown in the types, particularly in the sin offering. Before the animal was slaughtered, the sacrificing priest laid his hand upon its head (Lev. 4:3,4). That act represented the transferring of sin from the transgressor to the victim (Lev. 16:21): it identified the one with the other. It showed the substitution of the victim for the offender, and declared by a visible sign that it bare his sins and endured his death-penalty. In this way was the solemn yet blessed truth of IMPUTATION foreshadowed. It was because God* transferred to Christ the guilt of His elect, constituting Him **'sin for us,'** that the Sword of Divine Justice smote Him as He bare our sins in His own body on (or "to") the tree" (A.W. Pink). Jesus Christ has borne the sins of God's people on the accursed tree and carried them away forever. Christ has fully satisfied God's Justice, which demands death for sin: **"...The soul that sinneth it must die"** *(Ezek 18:4)*. What Christ, as High Priest of the election that is according to grace, has done is what the office of the high priest of the Old Testament foreshadowed He would do—**to make an atonement, or satisfaction, for the sins of all those whom God had directed Him to.** *"The Old Testament types supply incontrovertible evidence that the Gospel was no novel invention of New Testament times"* (A.W. Pink). *"From the time of the Fall, there has been but one way open to Heaven, and that was through Christ; and all believers, before and under the law, hoped for pardon of sin and salvation through Him. In hopes of that pardon and salvation they observed the typical services"* (W. Romaine). It is Christ Jesus the Lord, who makes a man free (Jn. 8:36), Who has paid the ransom price required for the freedom of all those whom the Father had given Him to die for. Man does not contribute to his freedom. It is not the hostage who pays the ransom: **"Even as the Son of man came not to be ministered unto, but to minister, and to give HIS LIFE a ransom for many"** *(Matt. 20:28)*. *"The Levitical sacrifices emphasized the enormity of sin and the punishment which must be visited upon it, as well as set forth the dependence of the forgiving grace of God on an expiatory offering....The principal thing they were designed to exhibit was the indispensable necessity of atonement by vicarious expiation"* (A.W. Pink). This simply means the death of a substitute, one who stood in the place of the offender to make amends for the sinner. **This shows conclusively that there was nothing in the sinner, or that the sinner could do, to make amends or restitution for his sin or sinfulness and dispenses with all arguments to the contrary.**

As we saw earlier, the high priest entered the holy of holies in order to make sacrifice for the people of Israel (Lev. 16:16,17). Sacrifice was not made for the Amelekites or the

Hittites nor was it made for the Egyptians or the Syrians or for any other nation on earth. God had not dealt with any other nation as He had with Israel: **"He sheweth His word unto Jacob, His statutes and His judgements unto Israel. He hath not dealt so with any nation: and as for His judgements, they have not known them. Praise ye the Lord"** *(Psa. 147:19,20).* God had decreed that sacrifice be made, an atonement be performed, for all the sins of every individual which made up the physical nation of Israel. **This would typify what the True and Great High Priest, Jesus Christ, would do for the SPIRITUAL nation of Israel: the election of grace.** *"The great sacrifice of Christ was foreshadowed from the beginning. He Who predestinated the salvation of His elect, did also appoint the means thereto: the Lamb* **'...verily was foreordained before the foundation of the world'** *(1 Pet.1:20; see also Rev. 13:8)...The Old Testament sacrifices were a 'showing forth of the Lord's death' till He came"* (A.W. Pink). **If one has a problem with this, then one has a problem with God.** It is no use arguing against this writer or any other person who teaches what God's Word says. The children of God are perfectly comfortable with their God Who does whatsoever He pleases. We may not fully understand all of what God does or why He does it, we are simply comfortable with the fact that God has done it. Again, the intricate details of what exactly the high priest did in the holy of holies, are not necessary to our study. What we are simply trying to show is **for whom** it was the duty of the high priest to make atonement for. The reason it is so important to know who the high priest made sacrifice for is that we are told in Scripture that the Old Testament high priest was merely a shadow, a type, a forerunner of the True and Only High Priest, the GREAT High Priest, Jesus Christ. **He pointed to the High Priesthood of the Messiah and what He would do.** What the Old Testament high priest did, was to show what THE True High Priest, Jesus Christ, would do. **Everything pointed to the ONE who would come.** When the high priest did what he did, God was in effect saying 'this is what My Son, Whom I have appointed the Great High Priest of all My elect whom I will give Him, will do.' **The Old Testament**

high priest and the New Testament High Priest, Jesus Christ, did what they did FOR THE PEOPLE OF GOD. The Old Testament high priest for the temporal people of God, the physical nation of Israel and the True Great High Priest for the eternal people of God, spiritual Israel, whom He has chosen from every nation on earth. It is imperative that we look to the Old Testament high priest in order to define and understand accurately the sacrificial terms of the Atoning work of the True High Priest, Jesus Christ. **Human reasoning will not reveal unto us the Wisdom of God** (1 Cor. 1:21)**–what He has done and for whom he has done it.** *"The plan of redemption, the office of our Surety, and the satisfaction which He rendered to the claims of justice against us, have no parallel in the relations of men to one another"* (Waymarks in the Wilderness, Vol. 6). God has in effect laid the blueprint down for us in the Old Testament, in order that we might understand aright what Christ would do in the New Testament. Any attempt to understand the atonement with human reasoning will lead one into deadly error and man-made doctrines and traditions.

So it is established from the many Scriptures which speak about the Old Testament high priest, his role and duties, that he did what he did under the direction of God for whom God had decreed he should do it—the nation of Israel, God's people. The role of the high priest was to be the representative of **God's people**. He was to do what he was appointed to do on behalf of the people of God. Atonement was not performed for anyone who was not part of God's people. **And, most importantly, atonement was not conditioned on a person's acceptance of what was done on his behalf before the atonement could take effect.** Atonement was not conditioned on a man's choice but was made by Divine appointment for those God had Sovereignly chosen. This is most important for it shuts down completely the blasphemous teaching that has permeated 99% of all religion, Roman Catholic or Protestant, that comes in the name of Christ, that Christ died for all and that salvation is conditioned on the sinner. This is one of the foundation teachings upon which is built a system wherein is taught that a man is to meet a condition/conditions before he can be saved. **It is a gospel by works, not of grace, and any who believe it are, at present, under the wrath of God** (see Gal. 1:8,9). As we shall see in the remaining pages of this booklet, the entire concept of such a teaching is so foreign, so absolutely and utterly alien to both the Old and New Testaments, as to reveal it for what it really is—**the Devil's doctrine!** To say that Christ has died for all, that is, made atonement for the sins of every single individual ever born, nullifies everything He did on the cross. **Deny Christ's work and you deny Him and the Father Who sent Him, for He prophesied what He would do** (Jn. 11:51,52). If Christ did atone for the sins of every single person, then every single person would be saved. The reason there is no other conclusion and why this is so absolutely irrefutable, is the fact that **atonement was never something that was conditioned on those for whom it was made. The Old Testament atonement was for God's people ONLY and this was the atonement which was the type of that which was to come.** It was not made for a people who it was hoped would one day become God's people, it was verily made for the elect people of God. Even pagan religion knows that it was the **sacrifice** made to the god which appeased the god and that it did not have a thing in the world to do with the people on whose behalf the sacrifice or appeasement was made. It is important to note the Divine origin of sacrifice: *"Whoever would have dreamed of the device of offering animal sacrifices to God as a method of acceptable worship? That Abel should have '**brought of the firstlings of his flock and of the fat thereof**' (Gen. 4:4), can only be satisfactorily accounted for on the ground that he knew this was what God required from him. And this is precisely what the New Testament affirms: Hebrews 11:4 declares that it was '**by faith**' that Abel offered his sacrifice, and Romans 10:17 says '**faith cometh by hearing, and hearing by the word of God.**' Thus, Abel had received a revelation from God, and believing what he had '**heard,**' acted accordingly. Moreover, the acceptance of Abel's sacrifice by a Divine testimony of approval (Gen. 4:4; Lev. 9:24; Judg. 6:21; 1 Kings 18;38) intimate the same thing"* (A.W. Pink). The high priest of the Old Testament, just as the true Great High Priest of the New Testament, Jesus Christ, was the representative of the people whom God had selected to be separate from the people of the world—a people not of the world but of God (Jn. 17:16). He went into the holy of holies and dared make sacrifice to the Holy God because he was directed by God to do so, and what the high priest did was between him and God for the benefit of God's people, exclusively. All that was done in the holy of holies was done for God's people and what was sought to be accomplished for His people, was completed in full once the atonement had been successfully presented. Extremely significant to this are the final words of Jesus Christ on the cross: **"It is finished"** (Jn. 19:30). Christ here was speaking of the great Atoning Sacrifice He had just performed on the behalf of all those whom He represented— the people whom God had given Him. (See Col. 2).

The word *'propitiation'* is vitally important to our study, for the meaning of this word adds significant weight to the fact that atonement was made for a specific number of people—the elect of God—and not for every individual ever born. Quite simply, the word *'propitiation'* means **satisfaction.** 1 John 2 teaches that Jesus Christ made propitiation, or satisfaction, for sins. This means that Christ as High Priest, the Representative of His people, which is made up of a predetermined number and not a number waiting to be determined upon the last saved man's 'choice' of God, made sacrifice to God on behalf of those people for whom He was to make atonement (just like the high priest was given a people to represent in the holy of holies). And that sacrifice of Christ, the Bible says, was SATISFYING TO A HOLY GOD (Eph. 5:2; Heb. 9:26,28). Christ went into THE Holy of Holies made without hands and obtained eternal redemption for His people because His sacrifice satisfied the demands of God's Holy Justice (Heb. 9:12; see also Col. 1:14). **"For Christ is not entered into the holy places made with hands, which are the figures of the true; but into Heaven itself, now to appear in the presence of God for us"** (Heb. 9:24). God's justice is now fully and forever satisfied. God's justice now demands no further penalty to be paid by the elect for their sin, for the penalty their sin had incurred has been fully met and paid for by the

Great High Priest, Jesus Christ (Heb. 10:12,14), on their behalf. **Satisfaction has been made.** Christ is the Satisfaction for His people and their sins. God demands nothing from the sinner in terms of payment—satisfaction of God's Justice—for sin: **"Now where remission of these is, there is no more offering for sin"** *(Heb. 10:18);* **"There is therefore now no condemnation to them which are in Christ Jesus, who walk not after the flesh, but after the Spirit"** (Rom. 8:1). To illustrate the atoning work of Christ and the satisfaction upon His death which was made to God's Justice, we turn to the Old Testament 'Passover', which was a type of the Promise God would make to all whose sins would be atoned for by Christ. *"The Divine promise* (to Israel) *was,* **'when I see the blood** (on the doorposts of their houses), *I* **will pass over you'** *(Ex. 12:13). The angel entered not such houses, for death had already done its work there—a substitute had been slain. Here is redemption, deliverance from judgement. God's design was to furnish a type of Christ,* (through the Passover lamb which was slain and whose blood was placed on the doorposts of the houses of the Israelites), *and instruct the faith of His people in things to come"* (A.W. Pink).

There is nothing that can be added to Christ's atoning work to make it more efficacious, for it was a perfect work and **God is fully satisfied with what Christ has done for all those whom He had given Him.** To even think that anything must be added to Christ's atonement, or that its efficaciousness is dependent or reliant on a worthless sinner, is the height of blasphemy. Listen to the apostle Paul: **"Behold, I Paul say unto you, that if ye be circumcised, Christ shall profit you nothing"** (Gal 5:2; see also Gal. 5:3-5). Paul is saying here that if a person claiming to have faith in Christ believes that they need to add even the smallest work of obedience to what Christ has done in order to either get saved or stay saved, then Christ shall in no way profit that person. In fact, the very next verse says: **"For I testify again to every man that is circumcised, that he is a debtor to do the whole law"** (Gal. 5:3; see also Gal. 3:10). Paul is saying that if a person has hope in anything that they have done which they believe was necessary for them to get saved or stay saved, that person is, according to God's Word, under obligation to obey the whole law perfectly or suffer the penalty of eternal damnation. If one is not convinced and cannot say that Christ's atonement **alone** was enough to meet the demands of God's justice in full and be content with that, then one cannot be a child of God for every child of God knows what has been done for him, what has been done on his behalf. **A Christian is not ignorant of the Person and Work of his Savior Jesus Christ, for how then could he trust in Him?** He has hope in Christ because he has heard the Gospel and now believes Who the Christ is and what He has done.

One must never forget the condition that sinful man is in: **Without God and therefore without hope in this world.** By works of the law shall no man be justified (Gal. 2:16). With man salvation is impossible (Matt. 19:26). Man, therefore, cannot do anything to recommend himself unto a Holy God. This is yet another nail in the coffin of those who say that salvation is conditioned on the sinner. Praise God salvation is not conditioned or dependant on the sinner in any way for we could not, indeed would not, ever come to God the Way He has prescribed if left to ourselves. The Lord Jesus Himself stated as much when He said: *"No man CAN come unto Me, EXCEPT THE FATHER which hath sent Me draw him..."* (Jn. 6:44). All of this fits comfortably with the teaching that, in order for a man to be made right with God, he needs a representative appointed by God to intercede, or act, on man's behalf. *"The law required sinless perfection (Deut. 27:10) under the penalty of eternal damnation, and thus it is revealed the imperative need of an atonement. While in Leviticus 16 we see how that law by its great sin-offering, with its blood atonement, pointed forward to Christ"* (A.W. Pink). That is what salvation is conditioned on. **Salvation is conditioned on the work of the One Who was chosen by God to represent man and do what God had appointed for Him to do on man's behalf, for man could never successfully represent himself.** It is only by Christ—Who He is and what He has done—that a man can approach the Holy God (Heb. 10:19-22). Therefore, every detail necessary to the salvation of a man was to be attended to, or fulfilled, by God Himself. Christ's Sacrifice, His atoning death, did not merely make salvation possible, **IT ACTUALLY AND TRULY ACCOMPLISHED SOMETHING!** *"However men may quibble and wrest the Scriptures, one thing is certain: The Atonement is no failure. God will not allow that precious and costly sacrifice to fail in accomplishing, completely, that which it was designed to effect. Not a drop of that holy blood was shed in vain. In the last great day there shall stand forth no disappointed and defeated Savior, but One who* **"shall see of the travail of His soul and be satisfied"** *(Isa. 53:11)"* (A.W. Pink). Christ successfully gained salvation, He obtained redemption, the Scripture tells us, for all of God's elect (Heb. 9:12): **"For if the blood of bulls and of goats, and the ashes of an heifer sprinkling the unclean, sanctifieth to the purifying of the flesh: How much more shall the blood of Christ, Who through the eternal Spirit offered Himself without spot to God, purge your conscience from dead works to serve the living God?"** (Heb. 9:13,14). God the Father has provided the Righteousness His chosen ones required and He has also provided the Sacrifice, the Lamb of God (Jn. 1:36), necessary to pay the price His people's sins had incurred. Many professing 'christians' today frown at a God who has provided salvation for 'only some, a select few' rather than making salvation possible for all if they would only choose Him, and yet strangely these same people are more than happy and comfortable with the God who chose Israel, to the exclusion of all others, to receive His great blessings in the Old Testament. However, true believers the world over rejoice in the God Who has provided salvation, not only for the elect of Israel, but for a people He has Sovereignly chosen from EVERY nation! Listen to how God answers after Moses requested to see God's glory: **"And He said, I will make all My Goodness pass before thee, and I will proclaim the Name of the Lord before thee; AND will be gracious to whom I will be gracious, and will shew mercy on whom I will show mercy"** (Ex. 33:18,19; see also Rom. 9:15-21).

    A powerful Scripture, found in the Letter to the Hebrews, teaches us so very clearly what exactly it was that set in motion the benefit of what every sinner chosen by God was to inherit. ***"And for this cause He*** (Christ) ***is the Mediator of the New Testament, THAT BY MEANS OF*** (His) ***DEATH, for the REDEMPTION of the transgressions that were under the first testament, THEY WHICH ARE CALLED might receive the promise of eternal inheritance. For where a testament is, there must also of necessity be the death of the testator"*** (Heb. 9:15,16). Here we see, that in order for redemption to take place, there must needs be a death. Blood must be shed in violent death, for therein is the life: ***"For the life of the flesh is in the blood: and I have given it to you upon the altar to make an atonement for your souls: for IT IS THE BLOOD THAT MAKETH AN ATONEMENT FOR THE SOUL"*** (Lev. 17:11) and ***"...without shedding of blood there is no remission*** (of sins)*"* (Heb. 9:22). In order for a last will and testament to be put into effect, there must needs be the death of the one who made it. It is not conditioned on the acceptance of what has been bequeathed by the testator, but what has been left a person becomes reality when the one who made the will dies. Jesus Christ has not only made sacrifice, or atonement, for God's people, HE IS THE SACRIFICE; HE IS THE ATONEMENT for all whom God chose. **God has promised an Inheritance for His people and it has now been put into force by the Death of His Beloved Son, Jesus Christ.** Therefore it is by means of **Christ's death** and **not the 'free-will' acceptance of it,** that has put into effect His last Will and Testament. The receiving of this great gift of salvation is, in reality, not a work of man's but the granting of a gift by God; it is the moment that God has appointed to open the eyes of one of His elect by His Holy Spirit through regeneration. Religion has always placed the emphasis on that precious moment (in time) when a man is saved, on man's choosing God, when in reality it is the granting and reception, by God's grace, of a Gift—the Gift of salvation. It is a presentation, by a loving God, to a vessel made willing by God to receive it: ***"Thy people shall be willing in the day of Thy Power..."*** (Psa. 110:3) and: ***"Blessed is the man whom THOU CHOOSEST, and CAUSEST to approach unto Thee..."*** (Psa. 65:4) It is God's work, not man's. **An elect man is merely a receptacle**

which God has chosen to be a vessel made unto honor, which He has filled with the water of everlasting life (Rom. 9:21-24). Can you begin to see how clear and simple all this really is? We are not to fear such subjects as the high priesthood of Christ. Every believer will know of His work as High Priest and rejoice in what has been done and achieved on his behalf by a loving Savior.

    I have had it verified for those who are not convinced by Scripture alone, by an independent source, namely a Jewish rabbi who is not a Christian, that the Old Testament plainly teaches that the high priest did what he did for the people of God **exclusively**, and that what he did was not dependant, or conditioned, on each individual's acceptance of what was done on their behalf, but the success of the atoning sacrifice depended solely on what the high priest did under the direction of God. Man, in his natural fallen state, is convinced by his highly deceitful and desperately wicked heart (Jer. 17:9), that if he does his best to serve and obey God, this will be pleasing to God and will result in his ultimate salvation. This is the sin that deceives every man by nature. **Man in his natural fallen state simply cannot accept the fact that there is nothing that he can do, or that he is to contribute, in order to gain favor with God.** And based on this flawed foundation, the lie has come about that Christ died for every individual, and the ultimate decision of whether a man goes to heaven or hell is left to man himself. **In other words, they say, it is not God Who makes the difference between saved and lost but the sinner himself.** This runs contrary to such Scriptures as Exodus 11:7: *"...the Lord doth put a difference between the Egyptians and Israel."* This has led to the controversy that what Christ, the true High Priest, has done is not merely for the nation of Israel, or for an elect people taken from every nation, but for the whole world, which most take to mean every single individual ever born. The false gospel teaches that salvation was not obtained by Christ on the cross, but that He has only succeeded in making it possible for every individual to receive salvation by his own free-will decision. This lie in turn does away with the fact that the Bible teaches that man is dead in sin, and replaces it with the satanic lie that man is not dead in sin but merely sin-sick and can, of his own free will, choose God with a little assistance from God, at any time. The Scripture asks: **"For who maketh thee to differ from another? And what hast thou that thou didst not receive?...."** (1 Cor. 4:7; see also Ex. 11:7). It is God that makes a saved man to differ from one who is lost. All that a saved man possesses has been given to him by a Sovereign God purely by grace and mercy. Even the faith by which a man believes is not of the man, but is of God (Eph.2:8). Man could do and has done nothing to recommend himself unto God and has contributed nothing in order to make himself differ from any other man (2 Tim. 1:9). As was stated earlier, such blasphemous teachings as Christ dying for every individual thus making salvation only possible and not effectual by His own atoning work on the cross, controverts all that is taught in Scripture about what atonement actually is. **The Bible knows nothing of an atonement made for sin which was dependant or conditioned on the sinner in any way, shape or form.** *"He who denies the penal and vicarious nature of Christ's death, repudiates the clear testimony of the types; he who sets aside the efficacy of His Sacrifice by reducing it to a merely 'making possible' the salvation of men does likewise, FOR THE TYPES KNOW NOTHING OF AN INEFFECTUAL SACRIFICE"* (A.W. Pink). Atonement in the Bible was always made for God's chosen people and not for any others. **No one becomes a child of God by anything they do.** It is all because of what God does. Election, satisfaction for sin, a perfect righteousness, the certainty that all whom God has chosen shall come to Him and remain with Him eternally, has all been the work of a Sovereign God performed on behalf of the sinner. **"For whom He did foreknow, He also did predestinate to be conformed to the image of His Son, that He might be the Firstborn among many brethren. Moreover whom HE did predestinate, them HE also called: and whom HE called, them HE also justified: and whom HE justified, them HE also glorified"** (Rom. 8:29,30).

The Scripture that most turn to in support of their argument that Christ died for all, that He made atonement for every individual ever born, is found in John's first letter:

"My little children, these things write I unto you, that ye sin not. And if any man sin, we have an Advocate with the Father, Jesus Christ the Righteous: And He is the Propitiation for our sins: and not for ours only but also for the sins of the whole world" (1 John 2:1,2). The words 'whole world' here are taken to mean every individual ever born. The teaching is that Christ has made atonement for the sins, not merely of the nation of Israel as the Old Testament high priest did, but for every individual of every nation in the entire world. Again, if one adheres to the biblical meaning of the word 'propitiation', we must say that if this were the case, then every man would be saved. Since it is clear that not every man becomes a believer in Jesus Christ and therefore that not all are saved, not all have had their sins forgiven based on the atoning work of the High Priest, Jesus Christ, Who in fact obtained eternal redemption, the forgiveness of sins, for all those for whom He made atonement, sacrifice, propitiation. The Bible clearly teaches that He ***"...entered in once into the holy place, having obtained eternal redemption for us"*** (Heb. 9:12). **The subtle lies of Satan are often boosted by a 'superficial understanding' of what the Scriptures say.** 1 John 2:2 does, on the surface, seem to support the view that Christ died for every individual. But the Scriptures are not something which we are to skim the surface of. We are to stop and dig, and search and study with diligence (2 Tim. 2:15). So often people go to Scripture trying to understand what is said with the modern-day use of English words instead of the biblical approach, which is comparing Scripture with Scripture, spiritual things with spiritual (1 Cor. 2:13).

What the apostle John is saying in His First letter is addressed to ***'my little children',*** which means he is addressing his words to those Jews who had believed on Jesus Christ. All believe that John was here writing to believers, but most fail to realize, conveniently in some cases, the significance of one very important little detail and that is that they were **JEWISH** believers. Proof of this can be found in such places as Galatians 2:9 where we are told that the apostle John, amongst others, was an apostle to the circumcision (i.e. Israel). What John was teaching here, and which may be found in the Gospel of John as well, may also be seen in the Book of Hebrews and other writings which were addressed to the Jews: that **the Messiah, the Christ who was to come and bring salvation for His people was not come only for those of Israel, but for the whole world, meaning people of every nation, the Gentiles, and not just the Jewish nation.** Paul the apostle made this plain for all to see and understand: **"And that He might make known the riches of His glory on the vessels of mercy, which He had afore prepared unto glory, even us, whom He hath called, NOT OF THE JEWS ONLY, BUT ALSO OF THE GENTILES"** (Rom. 9:23,24). This was a constant teaching throughout the New Testament.

"When John added (in 1 Jn. 2:2) *'and not for ours* (sins) *only, but also for the whole world,' he signified that Christ was the propitiation for the sins of the Gentile believers too, for...'the world' is a term contrasted with Israel* (throughout Scripture). *This interpretation is unequivocally established by a careful comparison of 1 John. 2:2 with John 11:51,52, which is a strictly parallel passage:* **'And this spake he not of himself: but being high priest that year, he prophesied that Jesus would die for that nation; And not for that nation only, but that also He should gather together in one the children of God that were scattered abroad.'** *Here Caiaphas, under inspiration, made known for whom Jesus should* **'die.'** *Notice now the correspondency of his prophecy with this declaration of John's:* (John): **"He is the Propitiation for our** (believing Israelites) **sins." "He prophesied that Jesus should die for that nation."** (John): **"And not for ours only."** (Caiaphas): **"And not for that nation only"** (John): **"But also for the whole world"**–that is, Gentile believers scattered throughout the earth" (Caiaphas): **"He should gather together in one the children of God that were scattered abroad"** (A.W. Pink). (See appendixes for more on *'propitiation'* and *'the whole world'.)*

"The proper meaning for the word for propitiation is that of reconciling, appeasing, turning away anger, rendering propitious or favorable. The idea is, that there is anger or wrath, or that something has been done to offend, and that *it is needful to turn away that wrath, or to appease."* **There no longer remains any wrath in God toward those for whom Jesus Christ is the Propitiation.** God has been propitiated, that is, His anger has been appeased and God's Justice is now fully satisfied in what Christ has done on behalf of all those He laid down His life for. There are many Scriptures which show quite plainly who those people were. God the Father has laid on God the Son all the sins of all His elect: *"...the Lord hath laid on Him the iniquity of us all"* (Isa. 53:6). Christ offered Himself to bear (carry away) the sins of His sheep: *"So Christ was once offered to bare the sins of many..."* (Heb. 9:28; see also Titus 2:14): *"And ye know that He was manifested to take away our sins..."* (1 Jn. 3:5; see also Matt. 1:21; Lk. 1:77). All the sins of all His people have been washed away in His own blood and are now removed as far as the east is from the west (Psa. 103:12): *"...Unto Him that loved US, and washed US from OUR sins in His own blood"* (Rev. 1:5). The penalty for the sins of all His people has been paid IN FULL FOR ALL TIME: *"...we are sanctified through the offering of the Body of Jesus Christ once for all"* (Heb. 10:10; Col. 2:13). Christ Jesus the Lord, Who is the Good Shepherd, said: *"I am the good shepherd: the good shepherd giveth His life for the sheep"* and *"...I lay down My life for the sheep"* (Jn. 10:11,15; see also 1 Cor. 5:7). That all of mankind are not referred to as sheep in the Bible is evident in the following Scriptures: *"And before Him shall be gathered all nations: and He shall separate them one from another, as a shepherd divideth his sheep from the goats: And He shall set the sheep* (from all nations) *on His right hand, but the goats on the left"* (Matt.25:32,33). The sheep spoken of here are those whom God has elected unto salvation. The damned are those described as goats (Matt. 25:34,41) and elsewhere as tares which the Devil, not God, has sewn (Matt. 13:38,39). The elect are also described as lost sheep and God searches for all of His lost sheep until He finds them and He delivers them, one and all, from judgement (Lk. 15:4 & Ezek. 34:11,12). Christ so loved the **Church** that He gave Himself exclusively for it: *"Husbands, love your wives, even as Christ also* *loved the Church, and gave Himself for it"* (Eph. 5:25; see also Acts 20:28) The Church, of course, is Christ's Bride made up of all God's elect. *"Who gave Himself for US, that He might redeem US from ALL iniquity, and purify unto Himself a peculiar* (special, one's own) *people, zealous of good works"* (Titus 2:14). In illustrating the love of God for His people, the apostle John, writing to Christians, said: *"...He laid down His life for US..."* (1 Jn. 3:16). And Paul the apostle, speaking to Christians, said: *"Christ hath redeemed US from the curse of the law, being made a curse for us..."* (Gal. 3:13). Christ took the blame for the sins of His people. He took the pain of suffering for their sins, which is why there is now **NO** condemnation to them which are in Christ Jesus (Rom. 8:1), they whom He suffered, made atonement, for. The following Scripture passage is crucial to a biblical understanding of who Jesus Christ has made atonement for: *"For verily He took not on Him the nature of angels; but He took on Him THE SEED OF ABRAHAM. Wherefore in all things it behoved Him to be MADE LIKE UNTO HIS BRETHREN, that He might be a merciful and faithful HIGH PRIEST in things pertaining to God, to make reconciliation for the sins of the people"* (Heb. 2:16,17). Who are the seed of Abraham? *"And if ye be Christ's, then are ye Abraham's seed, and heirs according to the promise"* (Gal. 3:29; see also Rom. 4:16). These are the seed of Abraham and Christ's brethren (Matt. 12:49,50). The **seed** are the **many** whom Christ Jesus came to save (Isa. 53:10,11). The called of God are a special people, God's own people, who will not experience the wrath of God, for the Lord Jesus laid down His life for them; He experienced God's wrath on the behalf of God's elect: *"Christ hath redeemed us from the curse of the law, being made a curse for us..."* (Gal 3:13; see also Isa. 53:10). *"For God hath not appointed US to wrath, but to obtain salvation by our Lord Jesus Christ, Who died for US..."* (1 Thess. 5:9,10; see also 1 Cor. 5:17). This verse shows clearly that Christ died representing all those whom God had not appointed to receive His wrath. The 'us' spoken of here clearly sets this group of people apart from those who have not been appointed by the Sovereign God to obtain salvation.

And these people have come to God, not by their own initiative, but because God has elected them from before the foundation of the world and predestinated them to obtain salvation made possible by the obedience and death of Jesus Christ, Who is their great High Priest. The elect have an appointment with salvation made by God Himself!

Since the Bible teaches that there is nothing that man can do by way of service or obedience to appease the anger and wrath of God which man's sins have incurred, the only hope of salvation which any man has is if God Himself would provide an appeasement, a satisfaction for His wrath and anger toward our sin. God has done this by appointing **a Representative of the people**, all those people whom He has elected unto salvation. Go back to Hebrews 9 and verse 15 and you will see that by means of His own death, the offering up of His own blood, Christ has obtained eternal redemption, not for every individual, but for ***"they which are CALLED".*** How can one possibly reconcile this verse with 1 John 2:2 if in fact Jesus Christ is the Propitiation for every sin of every individual ever born? Not to mention Scriptures such as Ephesians 5:25 where we are told that **Christ laid down His life, not for every individual, but for His Church which He loved to the exclusion of all others.** It is interesting to note that Christ's love for His Church is coupled with a commandment for men in Ephesians 5:25 to love their wives, **to the exclusion of all others**, just as Christ loved His Bride and gave Himself exclusively for her. There simply is no logic at all in the argument that Christ died for the sins of every individual ever born when one considers and is made aware of what the Bible teaches concerning the role of the high priest—**what he did and for whom he did it.** It is absolute nonsense to teach that Christ has atoned for the sins of every individual, that God is now satisfied, His wrath has been appeased and no more needs to be done except each individual's acceptance of what has been done and settled on his behalf! There is no Scriptural type, shadow, figure or precedent for such an 'atonement'. **Such teaching makes salvation conditioned on the sinner, which is another gospel, and would change God from a**

Sovereign Being Who does whatsoever He wills, to an impudent one who can only hope that His plans will go according to His will. It is nothing short of spiritual madness to hold to such inane convictions. It changes the whole message of God's Gospel from one of **'this is what God has done in saving a people for Himself'** to *'God has done His part and now we must do our part to make all that He has done effectual'*. Madness such as this has led the religious world to confess that hell is a monument to God's failure! This statement is agreed to by those of the Faith movement, right through to mainstream denominations who call themselves Protestant. Such blasphemy is unheard of in Scripture.

Again, the question is posed: *'If salvation is conditioned on the sinner and his choice of God, how on earth could man possibly do his part, that is accepting what has been done on his behalf, if he is dead in sin and dead to God and not capable of coming to God in the prescribed manner? All those to whom God gives the power to become sons of God and to believe on His name are those* **"Which were born, NOT of blood, NOR of the will of the flesh, NOR of the will of man, BUT OF GOD"** (Jn. 1:13). The Bible teaches that unless God draws a man to His Son, salvation is impossible (Jn. 6:44).There are some who say that God indeed does draw the man, He enables the man to come to Him, but unless this occurs, unless man does the coming, no salvation can take place. This is man-centered 'theology' and not what the Word of God teaches. **A MAN IS SAVED NOT BECAUSE HE HAS COME TO GOD BUT BECAUSE GOD HAS COME TO THE MAN.** Put simply, whenever one has salvation conditioned on the man doing something, **whether his doing it is attributed to God or not,** one has a gospel of works which cannot save (see Lk. 18:9-14).

Another matter which has escaped the attention of those who insist that Christ has died for all and has made satisfaction for all and their sins, is the fact that if Christ has made atonement for all the sins of every individual, would not this great atoning work also include covering the sin which causes man's greatest impediment in coming to God, that of unbelief? It is taught that God has done His part by providing a Savior, a High Priest who has made atonement for every sin of every individual ever born, and that the only thing that now needs to be done to make all this effectual, to make it real, is man coming to God. But would not every man come to God if Jesus was the Propitiation for all, **for the sin of unbelief would have been done away with!** Otherwise, we would have the situation that Jesus Christ has made atonement for every sin of every individual ever born, including the sin of unbelief, but that hell would, nevertheless, be full of people who died in unbelief, a sin that, along with man's other sins, was nailed to Christ's cross! **Surely God would not be so unjust as to have received payment for man's sins from Christ His Son and then demand that the sinner also make payment.** If all other sin has been atoned for, would it not be right in concluding that the sin of unbelief has also been taken out of the way? And, if not, then the sin of unbelief has not been done away with for **ANY** man and there is no atonement for it. The penalty it has incurred has not been paid and therefore no one can possibly come to God, for the sin of unbelief reigns supreme, being untouched by the blood of Christ. How ludicrous this all is in light of what God says in His Holy Word.

John Owen wrote the following: *"The Father imposed His wrath due unto, and the Son underwent punishment for, either: 1. All the sins of all men. 2. All the sins of some men, or 3. Some of the sins of all men. In which case it may be said: a. That if the last be true, all men have some sins to answer for, and so, none are saved. b. That if the second be true, then Christ, in their stead suffered for all the sins of all the elect in the whole world, and this is the truth. c. But if the first be the case, why are not all men free from the punishment due unto their sins? You answer, 'Because of unbelief.' I ask, Is this unbelief a sin, or is it not? If it be, then Christ suffered the punishment due unto it, or He did not. If He did, why must that hinder them more than their other sins for which He died? If He did not, He did not die for all their sins!"* If Jesus Christ has suffered the punishment for all the sins of every individual, would you think it fair for a Just and Holy God to again visit punishment upon those very same sins by sending people to hell for whom Christ has already paid the penalty? Has not Christ suffered the penalty of all sins, including the sin of unbelief? **If so, how could anyone for whom Christ has suffered, possibly die in unbelief when the penalty for that very sin of unbelief has already been paid by the Lord Jesus?** Those who insist that though Christ died for all the sins of all people, they will still go to hell if they do not choose Him, must live with the fact that this blind theology leaves them to conclude that a man who dies in unbelief must pay the price for his sins that Christ has already paid and appeased the wrath of Almighty God, and for which God's justice has no demands. I am sure that you can see the utter insanity of all this.

All this shows quite clearly that Christ has not put away the sins of every individual, but those sins alone which belonged to the elect of God. The Bible abounds with Scripture after Scripture which tells us that God has elected a people from every nation, not just the Jewish nation, to be His people (Rev. 5:9). Acts 3:25 spells it out plain and simple: *"Ye are the children of the prophets, and of the covenant which God made with our fathers, saying unto Abraham, And in thy seed shall ALL THE KINDREDS OF THE EARTH be blessed".* (see also Gen. 12:3; 18:18; 22:18; 26:4; Psa. 72:17). Galatians 3:8 also points out that people of every nation shall be saved: *"And the Scripture, foreseeing that God would justify the heathen through faith, preached before the Gospel unto Abraham, saying, In thee shall ALL NATIONS BE BLESSED."* Election is not according to any man's works but according to the grace of God alone. These elect ones from every nation have been given the Perfect Righteousness of Christ and have had their sins imputed (charged) to His account. Christ has nailed to His cross every sin of every person God the Father has given to Him and they are the ones who shall be saved: *"All that the Father giveth Me SHALL come to me; and him that cometh to Me I will in no wise cast out"* (Jn. 6:37). *"And you, (believers) being dead in your sins and the uncircumcision of your flesh, hath He quickened together with Him, having forgiven you all trespasses; Blotting out the handwriting of ordinances that was against us, which was contrary to us, and took it out of the way, nailing it to His cross"* (Col. 2:13,14). The elect are the chosen bride of Christ—chosen by the Father Himself.

Perhaps the best study of the work of Jesus Christ as the High Priest of His people is found in the Letter to the Hebrews. As in the Old Testament so it is in the New. God has appointed a Mediator between Himself and man. In the Old Testament it was between God and the nation of Israel, which was the **shadow** of the **substance** found in the New Testament, wherein God has appointed His Son to be the Mediator between Himself and His chosen people, which come from every nation, tribe and language. It is important to remember that the high priest's role as the mediatorial representative of God's people, was to represent a specific group of people to God, and to represent God to that specific group of people. The high priest did not do what he did for an unspecified or indeterminate number of people, upon whom depended the success of what the high priest would do. **Salvation is not conditioned on the sinner, for the sinner could never meet any of the conditions laid down by God.** There are conditions for salvation: **perfect obedience to God's law and perfect satisfaction of God's wrath towards our sins.** No man can meet either condition. That is why, if any man was to be saved, he needed a Mediator, a Liaison, a High Priest. Not a high priest taken from among sinful men, but a high priest who was perfect and sinless, sent of God. Jesus Christ is the One Whom God appointed and whose Priesthood is forever (Heb. 7:24). Christ needs not to repeat His sacrifice for the sins of His sheep yearly, as the Old Testament high priest did for the sins of Israel, because Christ's sacrifice was perfect (Heb. 7:26,27). The Blood of Christ satisfied all the demands of God's Justice and paid the penalty in full for all the sins of God's chosen ones. *"Be it known unto you therefore, men and brethren, that through this Man (Jesus) is preached unto you the forgiveness of sins: and by Him all that believe are justified from all things..."* (Acts. 13:38,39). *"But God commendeth His love toward us, in that, while we were yet sinners, Christ died for us. Much more then, being now justified by His blood, we*

shall be saved from wrath through Him" (Rom. 5:8,9; see also 1 Thess. 1:10; 5:9). The Bible says we are fully reconciled to God by the death of His Son (Rom. 5:10). **NO wrath remains for the sins for which Christ has suffered.** Someone wisely said:: **"Jesus Christ has drunk damnation dry"** for every sinner for whom He died.

Christ Jesus the High Priest, the Mediatorial Representative of His people, is able to save and does save all those who come to God by, or through, Him: ***"Wherefore He is able also to save them to the uttermost that come unto God by Him, seeing He ever liveth to make intercession for them"*** (Heb. 7:25). Christ says that no man can come to the Father but by Him (Jn. 14:6) and that no man can come to Him unless the Father draws him (Jn. 6:44). The elect are made up of all those who believe in the Gospel of Jesus Christ, who in turn are: all those who have been drawn by the Father to the Son: all who come to the Father by Jesus Christ: all whom the Father has given His Son. Christ makes intercession for all those who come to God by Him and for whom He has made atonement. The Bible says that all who come to Him are all the ones whom God has given Him: ***"All that THE FATHER GIVETH ME shall come to Me; and him that cometh to Me I will in no wise cast out"*** (Jn. 6:37). Yes, a man must come to God to be saved, but this is not a condition that the man must meet in order to 'get saved', it is the evidence that he **is saved,** a chosen vessel made unto honor. **It is God that causes the man to approach unto Him and nothing within the man. So to be biblically accurate in our definition of salvation, we should say that it is God coming to man.** A man only comes to God because God came to him **first**. God is the Initiator. Man loves God because God loved him first etc. (1 Jn. 4:10,19).

The high priest was the only one permitted by God to enter the holy of holies. This was done only once a year on the great Day of Atonement. ***"But into the second went the high priest alone once every year, not without blood, which he offered for himself, and for the errors of the people"*** (Heb. 9:7). The blood was the blood of animals which was presented to God in order to atone for the sins of the people, the nation of Israel. This was merely a shadow of what was to come. Christ offered up, not the blood of animals which could never take away sins eternally (Heb.10:11), but His very own precious blood for the sins of the people, God's people, elect from every nation. **"Neither by the blood of goats and calves, but by His own blood He entered in once into the holy place, having obtained eternal redemption for us"** (Heb 9:12). Now the 'us' mentioned here could not possibly mean every individual in the entire world, for then all would be saved seeing that eternal redemption has been obtained for the 'us'. The preaching of the Gospel is unto the Jews a stumblingblock and foolishness unto the Greeks (Gentiles) **"but UNTO THEM WHICH ARE CALLED, both Jews and Greeks, Christ the power of God, and the wisdom of God"** (1 Cor. 1:23,24). Obviously the 'us' here refers immediately to the writer and his believing hearers, but also to all those whom Christ, the Great High Priest, represented: all whom God had given Him to represent, the called who make up the whole election of grace! Such is the case in John 17:20: **"Neither pray I for these alone, but for them also which shall believe on Me through their word"** and John 10:16: **"And other sheep I have, which are not of this fold** (the Jewish fold)**: them also I must bring, and they shall hear My voice: and there shall be one fold, and one Shepherd."** Notice that Christ says there are other sheep He **HAS**, not would have. Christ already considered those for whom He would die, His very sheep.

      Here again is one of the most significant verses in all of Scripture pertaining to what Jesus Christ has done and for whom He has done it: **"And for this cause He** (Christ Jesus) **is the Mediator of the New Testament, that by MEANS OF DEATH, for the REDEMPTION of the transgressions that were under the first testament, THEY WHICH ARE CALLED might receive the promise of eternal inheritance"** (Heb. 9:15). We see here that it is by means of the atoning death, sacrifice or offering of Jesus Christ which was made for a specific purpose which this verse tells us was for the redemption of a particular people: **the called of God.** There is nothing here which speaks of redemption for the whole world, but **the Scripture explicitly teaches REDEMPTION THROUGH THE MEANS OF CHRIST'S DEATH FOR THE CALLED OF GOD ALONE!** That **THEY,** not every individual in the whole world, but **THEY, THE CALLED OF GOD,** might receive the promise of eternal inheritance.

The following verses in Hebrews 9 talk about the death of the testator, the one who has made a last will and testament, which puts the will into effect. It is by means of his death that one receives what has been bequeathed or promised. The will has no strength while the testator lives. If you have made a will or are thinking of making one, what you will to a person does not become theirs until your death, which is what puts into effect the promises made in your will. Who will you leave your belongings to? **Would it not be an act of an unsound mind to leave one's belongings to anyone who will accept them and not to those who are one's very own children?** A will, in normal circumstances, is made out to the nearest kin, usually a son or daughter. No sane person would comment that the person who died was unfair to leave his fortune to his son or daughter and not to as many people as he could have. I will bequeath my belongings to my son and God has promised all that He has, in fact His very Self, to His own children, the children of election: **"The Lord is the Portion of mine inheritance ..."** (Psa. 16:5; see also Ezek. 44:28). This is a perfectly just and right thing to do and anyone who would argue against what God has done is a lost man. God may do with us as the potter with the clay (Rom. 9:18-21 & Jer.18:6). If I may use such course terminology, **God has not prostituted Himself by making Himself available to anyone who will accept Him as long as they agree to His terms. God has PROMISED Himself in covenant love to all His elect, His inheritance.**

"...but now once in the end of the world hath He (Christ) *appeared to put away sin by the sacrifice of Himself. So Christ was once offered to bear the sins of many* (not all)*; and unto them that look for Him shall He appear the second time without sin unto salvation"* (Heb. 9:26,28). Again, we see that Christ, by His sacrifice, has put away sin. **This includes the sin of unbelief.** If all

this means that what Christ has done is to merely remove the sin problem and gotten it out of the way so as to **make possible** the salvation of all men as long as they believe, then all would come to salvation for the ultimate sin blocking man's way to God, that of unbelief, has been dealt with! To subscribe to such a teaching is to reveal one's status of spiritual lostness. **Christ has done away with every sin of all whom God has given Him to represent.** Christ has borne, carried away, the sins of many—**His seed**— not all (Isa. 53:10, 11). The 'many' here referred to are the many whom God has elected to be saved. Those who look for Christ are those whose sins He has borne, those whom the Father has drawn to His beloved Son. In reality, they are the ones for whom God is searching and whom He will deliver from darkness to Light (Acts 26:17,18): ***"For thus saith the Lord God; Behold, I, even I, will both search My sheep, and seek them out. As the shepherd seeketh out his flock in the day that he is among his sheep that are scattered; so will I seek out My sheep, and will deliver them..."*** (Ezek. 34:11,12; see also Lk. 15:4,5); ***"For by one offering He hath perfected for ever them that are sanctified"*** (Heb.10:14). All that Christ has done in His Office of High Priest, has been done for those who are sanctified. The word 'sanctified' here, as in the rest of the New Testament, means 'to make holy, purify or consecrate'. Christ has perfected eternally all those whom God has chosen to make holy (vessels unto honor), and whom He has purified.

      The Letter to the Hebrews is written to believers. Throughout it, and many other books in the New Testament, you will see the words *'us', 'we'* and other such references. So it is here, in Hebrews 10, that the writer refers to Christians. Words such as *'we', 'us'* or *'ourselves'* etc., **never include unbelievers.** Saved people are never grouped in with the unbelievers of the world, but are always spoken of separately and distinctly from the lost, after salvation, for God deals in a special way with those whom He has chosen. **It is called GRACE.** We—Christians—are an eternally separated people unto God, chosen before the foundation of the world to be separate from the world of unbelievers and predestinated to become His children, whose sins were atoned for by His only Begotten Son in the sacrifice of His precious Blood upon the tree. In the Old Testament the high priest made atonement, that is, brought a sacrifice unto God, to cover the sins of all Israel, not all the world. All for whom this was done gained forgiveness from God. So, too, the Great High Priest, Jesus Christ, has made atonement for all His people elected from every nation before the foundation of the world. **ALL FOR WHOM THIS WAS DONE SHALL BE SAVED, AND THAT ETERNALLY** (Heb. 9:12-14).

APPENDIX A

THE SATISFACTION OF CHRIST: IT'S TYPIFICATION

(The following is taken from chapter 21 of the book 'Studies in the Atonement', by A.W. Pink)

Christ has been greatly dishonored and His atonement grievously misrepresented by the attempts which have often been made to illustrate it from supposed analogies in human relations. Rightly has it been said that, "The plan of redemption, the office of our Surety, and the satisfaction which He rendered to the claims of justice against us, have no parallel in the relations of men to one another. We are carried above the sphere of the highest relations of created beings into the August counsels of the eternal and independent God. Shall we bring *our* own line to measure *them*? We are in the presence of Father, Son and Holy Spirit; one in perfections, will and purpose. If the righteousness of the Father demands a sacrifice, the love of the Father provides it. But the love of the Son runs parallel with that of the Father; and not only in the general undertaking, but in every act of it we see the Son's full and free consent" (*Waymarks in the Wilderness, Vol. 6*).

But while no parallel to the Great Transaction, or to the relation of the Father, Son and Holy Spirit to its accomplishment, can be found in any of the relations of mere creatures to one another, God has graciously adapted a series of *types*, historical and ceremonial, to the illustration of His wondrous plan, and especially to portray the various aspects of the office and work of Christ. In them the Divine wisdom is signally displayed, and it is the part of human wisdom to devote our closest attention to the same. By the typical system, God was not only educating His people for the "good things to come," but was also preparing human language to be a fit medium for the revelation of His grace in Christ. It is to the types we must turn if we would define aright the sacrificial terms of the New Testament.

But an impression obtains in some quarters that instruction by the types belongs to an inferior dispensation, and was only designed for the Church in the days of its infancy. Scripture teaches otherwise. It is true that "the typology of the Pentateuch is the Divine kindergarten," yet it is also true that "Whatsoever things were written aforetime were written for *our* learning (Rom. 15:4), and that God's dealings with Israel were "our types" (1 Cor. 10:6 margin). Yea, so far from the study of the types being an elementary one, Hebrews 5:10-12 shows that they furnish our "strong meat."

While it is true that the "typology of the Pentateuch is the Divine kindergarten," this does not mean either that the teaching of the types is to be lightly esteemed, or that the instruction which they furnish is inferior in quality to that which is given in the Epistles. No schoolchild is really qualified to take in the teaching of the higher grades until he is thoroughly familiar with and has more or less mastered the lessons of the lower grades. So none are fully equipped to receive the evangelical teachings of the New Testament, if the key-phrases of the old Testament types are neglected. Not only has the sacrificial work of Christ as many aspects as there are great sacrifices in the Pentateuch, but the doctrinal statements of the Epistles are frequently couched in the language of the types, and can only be rightly interpreted in the light which they furnish.

"A type is something emblematic or symbolic, used to express, embody, represent or forecast, some person, truth or event. It is an image or similitude of something else, sustaining to doctrinal teaching some such relation as a picture does to a precept or promise, presenting to the eye or imagination a concept addressed to the ear or understanding. It is one of the most frequent forms of figurative teaching in Scripture, but being sometimes more obscure than obvious demands keener insight and closer study" (A.T. Pierson). The types were prophecies, forecasts of things to come, and therefore do they furnish one of the most striking and conclusive proofs of the Divine inspiration of the Scriptures, for only He Who knew the end from the beginning could have so accurately, so fully, and so marvellously anticipated and adumbrated Calvary thousands of years before Christ died.

"The Old Testament types were a mode of instruction of the way in which God was to be approached, and were peculiarly suited to the human mind struggling with a sense of guilt; and they have furnished to the Church of all times, a vocabulary or nomenclature, without which men could not with sufficient precision have been able to hold intercourse with each other on the subject of the Atonement. It deserves special notice that prophecy and the sacrifices are always found together, and throw light upon each other; and that they run in parallel lines through the entire Old Testament economy. Nay, the sacrifices may be regarded as a sort of prophecy, or a guarantee to which the veracity of God was pledged, for the shadow must one day be a reality" (Geo. Smeaton). "A type is a prophetic symbol, and since prophecy is a prerogative of Him who sees the end from the beginning, a real type, implying as it does a knowledge of the Reality, can only proceed from God" (Liddon's Bampton Lectures).

The Old Testament types supply incontrovertible evidence that the Gospel was no novel invention of New Testament times. When the risen Savior would make known to His disciples the meaning of His death, we read that, "Beginning at Moses and all the prophets, He expounded unto them in all the Scriptures the things concerning Himself" (Lk. 24:27). So far from the evangel of the apostle's being any (absolutely) new thing, every element in it was revealed long centuries before their birth, not only in words, but in visible representations: there was both a wondrous anticipation of and preparation for the Gospel. Thus a reverent contemplation of the types supplies a blessed confirmation of faith, for they attest the Divine Authorship of both Testaments. Moreover, they stimulate adoration, even when we know a person, we enjoy looking at his picture; so here. It is *Christ* that is before us in them.

The *Divine* origin of sacrifice is self-evident. Whoever would have dreamed of the device of offering animal sacrifices to God as a method of acceptable worship? That Abel should have "brought of the firstlings of his flock and of the fat thereof" (Gen. 4:4), can only be satisfactorily accounted for on the ground that he knew this was what God required from him. And this is precisely what the New

Testament affirms: Hebrews 11:4 declares that it was: "by faith" that Abel offered his sacrifice, and Romans 10:`17 says "faith cometh by hearing, and hearing by the word of God." Thus, Abel had received a revelation from God, and *believing* what he had "heard," acted accordingly. Moreover, the acceptance of Abel's sacrifice by a Divine testimony of approval (Gen. 4:4), which, no doubt, was given by the descent of consuming fire from heaven—Leviticus 9:24; Judges 6:21; 1 Kings 18:38—intimate the same thing. *That solemn testimony of reception would only have terrified the offerer, had he himself invented this mode of worship! "The lightning shooting round the altar, and consuming the victim, would have conveyed the impression of an angry God: how, then, could they have apprehended by this means that they were reconciled? How could they have know without a Divine revelation that this consuming fire was a token of Divine acceptance?" (*G. Smeaton*).*

The great sacrifice of Christ was foreshadowed from the beginning. He Who predestinated the salvation of His elect, did also appoint the means thereto: the Lamb was "foreordained before the foundation of the world" (1 Pet. 1:20). Then what memorial could be devised more opposite than that of animal sacrifices? By such a means was exemplified the *death* which had been denounced upon man's disobedience, and in the shedding of the victim's blood and the violent character of its death, was portrayed something of the awfulness of that death which was the "wages of sin." At the same time a fit representation was also made of that death that was to be undergone by the Redeemer, and thus there was connected in one view the two cardinal facts in the history of men—the *fall* and *recovery* from it. The Old Testament sacrifices were a "showing forth of the Lord's death till He came."

It is both important and blessed to note that the Gospel-covenant was revealed by God immediately after the Fall. The promise that the woman's Seed should bruise the serpent's head (Gen. 3:15) and the institution of the types (Gen. 3:21), were to the very end that faith and hope might be preserved in what God had so graciously purposed. God did not leave even our first parents in ignorance of His merciful designs, but made known the nature of His eternal counsels. Soon after, a further revelation was made unto Cain and Abel, and still later to others. The infinite wisdom of God so contrived the types that they might in the most intelligible manner (that material things can describe spiritual) signify the Redeemer, and life and salvation through Him. "From the time of the fall, there has been but one way open to Heaven, and that was through Christ; and all believers, before and under the law, hoped for pardon of sin and salvation through Him. In hopes of that pardon and salvation they observed the typical services" (W. Romaine).

That the Old Testament saints perceived something at least of the mystical and spiritual meaning of the types is clear from a number of passages; that they had a much clearer and fuller apprehension of them than is commonly supposed, is the writer's firm conviction. The Lord Jesus declared that "Abraham rejoiced to see My day: and he saw, and was glad" (Jn. 8:56) Hebrews 11:13 tells us that the patriarchs confessed themselves to be "strangers and pilgrims on the earth," which shows they knew that their true "inheritance" was in Heaven; while Hebrews 11:14, 16 expressly states they sought and desired "an heavenly" country. Job said, "I know that my Redeemer liveth" (19:25), and the Hebrew word there for "Redeemer" signifies one who is a redeemer by right of affinity or kinship—not only a Redeemer in act, but in office. So also David acknowledged, "my flesh longeth for Thee...to see Thy power and Thy glory, so as I *have seen* Thee in the sanctuary" (Psa. 63:2), that is, by means of the figures and shadows of the vessels of the tabernacle and the Levitical services and sacrifices.

"First the blade, then the ear and then the full corn in the ear" enunciates one of the principles of Divine work in everything, the types not excepted. The further we proceed, the profounder their meaning, and the fuller their detail. In the Divine clothing of our first parents with "coats of skins" (Gen. 3:21), there were illustrated the facts that: fallen man needed an external covering to fit him to stand before God; that he could not produce this by his own labors; hat the life of an innocent victim must be taken, in order to provide a suitable covering for him; that God Himself must provide it.

In the offering of Abel and God's acceptance of the same (Gen. 4:4), we learn that God can only regard any sinner with favor by virtue of his acceptance in Christ. The *Divine* origin of sacrifices is again intimated in that before flesh was eaten by man, the distinction between clean and unclean animals was quite familiar (Gen. 8:20). The power of an accepted sacrifice to remove the *Divine* curse was plainly signified in Genesis 8:21. The principle of substitution was strikingly manifested in Genesis 22:13.

What may be termed the first *great* sacrifice was the "Passover," recorded in Exodus 12. There we behold the efficacy of the lamb's precious blood to deliver those sheltering beneath it from that judgement of God which their sins deserved. What virtue, an infidel might ask, had the blood of a poor animal to secure the life of Israel's first-born from the sword of a mighty and invisible angel? Was the blood on the door a necessary mark for the angel, because he had not understanding enough to distinguish between the houses of Egyptians and Israelites? Could not God have signified His pleasure to the angel without such a mark as that? The answer to these, and all such questions is, God's design was to furnish a type of *Christ*, and instruct the faith of His people in things to come.

The following is a bare outline of the point in the Passover-type which may be profitably studied by the reader. First, Divine judgement was pronounced: "*all* the firstborn [the representative of the family] *in* [not of] the land of Egypt shall die" (Ex. 11:5). Second, God "put a difference between the Egyptians and Israel" so that not one of His own people were hurt (Ex. 11:7). Third, not by Israel's choice or Moses recommendation, but by Divine appointment every Israelitish household was to take an unblemished lamb, kill it, and apply its blood to the outside of his house (Ex. 12:3-7). Fourth, the Divine promise was, "when I see the blood, I will pass over you" (Ex. 12:13). Fifth, the angel entered not such houses, for death had *already* done its work there—a substitute had been slain. Here is *redemption*; deliverance from judgement.

At Sinai God made known His will much more fully respecting the sacrifices which He required. A great deal of instruction therein is to be found in the first seven chapters of Leviticus, into most of which we cannot now enter: much deeply important teaching is to be found therein in a typical form. The Levitical sacrifices emphasized the enormity of sin and the punishment which must be visited upon it, as well as set forth the dependence of the forgiving grace of God on an expiatory offering. Under the Mosaic economy an elaborate system was developed to show that in many ways man offends God and is worthy of death. The sacrifices vividly evidenced the fact that the Divine punishment incurred was inevitable, yet that that punishment could be borne by a substitute, and on that ground the offender could be restored to favor. The principal thing they were designed to exhibit was the indispensable necessity of atonement by vicarious expiation: the one great truth they illustrated was that God could not sacrifice His holiness to His love.

That the Mosaic sacrifices all pointed forward to Christ and had their end in Him, was evidenced by the fact that very soon after He had come and shed His blood, God caused the shadows to pass away. Within a very few years the temple was destroyed, and with it all the Jewish sacrifices ceased. And though a century or two later Julian the Apostate gave the Jews permission to build heir temple, and that for the very purpose of restoring the ancient rites, yet God from Heaven blasted all their attempts in a miraculous and extraordinary manner.

The Levitical sacrifices made clear to men the ground on which the Divine pardon could be obtained. It was not an act of absolute mercy, nor was it bestowed on the sole condition of penitence, but on the consideration of something quite distinct from both. "And it shall be, when he shall be guilty in one of these things, that he shall confess that he hath sinned in that thing. And he shall bring his trespass offering unto the Lord for his sin...and the priest shall make an atonement for him concerning his sin...and it shall be forgiven him" (Lev. 5:5,6,10). If we compare these verses with Leviticus 17:11, which informs us that it is the blood which maketh an atonement for the soul", then the proof is conclusive that the sacrifice presented by the offender was the appointed means of obtaining forgiveness for his transgression.

The burnt offering (Lev. 1) and the sin offering (Lev. 4) claim particular attention, for not only were *they* the most important sacrifices of the Levitical dispensation (as Psalm 40:6 intimates), but they represented the sufferings of our great High Priest under two distinct aspects. The burnt offering principally shows Christ as he was to God, the sin offering as He is to men. In both He was represented as a sin-bearer, for in both of these sacrifices transfer was made of sin by the priest laying his hand on the head of the victim (Lev. 1:4; 4:4); in both the victim's blood was shed and sprinkled (Lev. 1:5; 4:4-6); in both atonement was made for sin (1:4; 4:20); and both were burnt, either wholly or in part upon the altar (1:9; 4:9,10). These points of union were sufficiently close to show that they corresponded in representing the sacrifice offered by our High Priest on the cross.

But there were also distinctive differences between them of a character sufficiently marked to show that they represented Christ's sacrifice under *different* aspects. Thus, the burnt offering was voluntary (Lev.1:2,3), the sin offering compulsory (Lev. 4:2,3). The burnt offering was flayed, cut into pieces, and the inwards and legs washed in water; but none of these things were required of the sin offering. The blood of the burnt offering was merely sprinkled round about upon the altar (1:1), but the blood of the sin offering was put upon the horns of the altar, sprinkled seven times before the Lord, before the veil of the sanctuary, and poured out at the bottom of the altar of burnt offering (4:6,7). Other differences we now pass over, desiring to direct attention merely to the first one mentioned.

The *voluntariness* of Christ's death is clearly brought out in Psalm 40:7,8 and Ephesians 5:25; John 10:17,18 also shows He freely laid down His life for His sheep. But, when in the councils of eternity ratified by the everlasting covenant "ordered in all things and sure," Christ had undertaken to be our Surety, *then* what was before purely free and voluntary became in a sense *compulsory*. Just as when God binds Himself by oath, He is obliged to fulfill His word, so Christ once He had bound Himself to stand in His peoples' place and stead, was no longer free—though, not that He wished to be free. Just as the type was bound with cords "unto the horns of the altar" (Psa. 118:27), so Christ was held fast to the Cross not only by love to His people, which floods could not quench, but by His own eternal covenant-engagement.

The substitution of Christ in the sinner's place was most distinctly shown in the types, particularly in the sin offering. Before the animal was slaughtered, the sacrificing priest laid his hand upon its head (Lev. 4:3,4). That act represented the transferring of sin from the transgressor to the victim (Lev. 16:21): it identified the one with the other. It showed the substitution of the victim for the offender, and declared by a visible sign that it bare his sins and endured his death-penalty. In this way was the solemn yet blessed truth of *imputation* foreshadowed. It was because God transferred to Christ the guilt of His elect, constituting Him "sin for us," that the sword of Divine justice smote Him as He bare our sins in His own body on (or "to") the tree.

The most important of all the types is that which is found in Leviticus 16: the appointed ritual for the great day of atonement. The type of Leviticus 16 goes much farther than does the one in Exodus 12: the Passover illustrated the *redemptive* character of Christ's sacrifice; that of Leviticus 16 its *propitiatory* nature. In Exodus 12 we see the blood sheltering from judgement those who are under it; in the early chapters of Leviticus, we see the power of the blood restoring to communion the penitent transgressor; but in Leviticus 16 we behold the blood opening a way into the very presence of God, entitling the penitent and believing worshipper to come with boldness unto His very Throne.

By a careful comparison of Deuteronomy 27 and Leviticus 16 we may discover how the law was, and still is, a "schoolmaster" unto Christ (Gal. 3:24). In the former chapter, we see that the law demanded implicit and complete obedience to its demands (v. 10); and how that the Levites pronounced with "a loud voice" a *curse* on the transgressor of it (vv. 14,15). That curse was repeated twelve times, according to the number of Israel's tribes, and on each pronouncement thereof "all the people" were required to say "Amen": the final word being "Cursed be he that confirmeth not all the words of this law to do them" (v.26)—cf. Galatians

3:10. The law required sinless perfection under the penalty of eternal damnation, and thus it revealed the imperative need of an *atonement*. While in Leviticus 16 we see how that law by its great sin-offering, with its blood of atonement, pointed forward to Christ.

The sacrificial system of Judaism reached its climax on the great day of atonement. As the ark was the chief object in the tabernacle, so the annual Day of Propitiation was the chief one in Israel's religious calendar. On that auspicious occasion the high priest divested himself of his robes of "glory and beauty" (Ex. 28), and put on "the holy linen" garments (Lev. 16:4). The spotless white in which he was clothed spoke of the perfect *righteousness* of Christ, which, tested as it was both by man (John 8:46) and Satan (John 14:30), and then passing through the infinitely searching scrutiny of God under the fiery trial of the cross, insured the Divine acceptance of that satisfaction which He made to God on behalf of His people.

Two young goats were selected "for a sin-offering;" though there were two animals, it was but one offering. Two goats were selected in order that a fuller representation might be given: the one being designed more expressly to exhibit the *means* the other the *effect* of the atonement. They were brought and presented together before the Lord (v. 7), the Lord determining by lot which of them was to be slain. The other animal stood by and was atoned for (Hebrew of verse 10) by he dying victim, and then bore away the sins laid upon it into the land of eternal forgetfulness (vv.21,22): a blessed figure of that *remission* of our sins when we believe on the Lord Jesus Christ unto salvation.

Passing by what was done with the bullock, e confine our attention to the two goats. After the one had been killed, the high priest took its blood within the veil and sprinkled it upon the mercy- seat not once, but seven times "before" Him to provide a *perfect* standing ground for His people. The antitype of this is seen in Hebrews 9:12, "But by His own blood He entered in once into the holy place, having obtained eternal redemption" (Heb. 9:12). The consequence of this is that "Having therefore, brethren, boldness to enter into the holiest by the blood of Jesus, by a new and living way which He hath consecrated for us" (Heb. 10:19,20).

After the high priest has finished his work inside the sanctuary, we are told, "he shall bring the live goat, and Aaron shall lay both his hands upon the head of the live goat and confess over him all the iniquities of the children of Israel...and shall send him away by the hand of a fit man into the wilderness: and the goat shall bear upon him all their iniquities into a land not inhabited" (vv.20-22). That was a continuation and completion of the ceremony concerning the sin-offering, so that this symbolic transfer of their sins to the head of the scapegoat, which bore them away, plainly signified that the atonement effected by the sacrifice of the first goat was the complete removal of all their transgressions from before the face of God.

"And Aaron shall come into the tabernacle of the congregation, and shall put off the linen garments, which he put on when he went into the holy place, and shall *leave* them there" (Lev. 16:23). Why? To denote that his work was *finished*. The blessed antitype of this we see in Luke 24:12: on the resurrection morning, those who came to Christ's empty sepulchre "beheld the *linen clothes*" lying there, a token that He was risen from the dead, and so of atonement completed, and accepted by God.

One other important feature in the types, often overlooked, claims our notice, namely, the *burning* of the victim's body on the altar (Lev. 1:10 etc.). The animal was first slain as a just judgement for the sin which had been transferred to it by the laying on its head of the hand of the offerer; and then, after guilt had been borne, its flesh was laid on the altar and burned, and went up with acceptance unto God, a "sweet smelling savor." In this was represented the glorious truth that, not only was Christ our sin-bearer, but that He is also our *righteousness* before God (Jer. 23:6; 2 Cor. 5:21). We are identified with Him not only in His *death* for us, but also in the *fragrance* of it before God.

In Numbers 19 there is yet another most important type upon which we can only now say a few words. In it we see how the death of Christ has made full provision for those defilements which His people contract while passing through this evil world. In it too we behold again the steady progress in the types, and the deeper instruction which God gave to Israel from time to time. They were yet in the land pf Pharaoh when the passover was instituted: the doom of Egypt and their own deliverance therefrom were the thoughts then presented to their souls. Later, they were brought nigh to God, Himself tabernacling in their midst, and in Leviticus 16 they are shown the high demands of His holiness. Now in Numbers 19, they are taught that even the unavoidable contact with death (the world lying in the Wicked one) defiles. But God has provided cleansing from it.

In closing, we call attention to one other deeply important value of the types and the use to which they may be put: they furnish an infallible rule by which can be *tested* any man's (our own included) *interpretation* of the New Testament Scriptures concerning the Atonement! He who denies the penal and vicarious nature of Christ's death, repudiates the clear testimony of the types; he who sets aside the efficacy of His sacrifice by reducing it to a merely "making possible" the salvation does likewise, for the types know nothing of an ineffectual sacrifice. So too in them we see plainly the *limitation* of God's love to His elect people, for no lamb was provided for the Egyptians, nor did Aaron make any atonement for the sins of the Midianites and Ammonites!

APPENDIX B

1 JOHN 2:2

(The following is an article by A.W. Pink)

THERE is one passage more than any other which is appealed to by those who believe in universal redemption, and which at first sight appears to teach that Christ died for the whole human race. We have therefore decided to give it a detailed examination and exposition.

"And He is the propitiation for our sins: and not for ours only, but also for the sins of the whole world" (1 Jn. 2:2). This is the passage which, apparently, most favors the Arminian view of the Atonement, yet if it be considered attentively it will be seen that it does so only in appearance, and not in reality. Below we offer a number of conclusive proofs to show that this verse does not teach that Christ has propitiated God on behalf of all the sins of all men.

In the first place, the fact that this verse opens with "and" necessarily links it with what has gone on before. We, therefore, give a literal word for word translation of 1 John 2:1 from Bagster's Interlinear: "Little children my, these things I write to you, that ye may not sin; and if anyone should sin, a paraclete we have with the Father, Jesus Christ (the) righteous". It will thus be seen that the apostle John is here writing *to* and *about* the *saints* of God. His immediate purpose was two-fold: first, to communicate a message that would keep God's children from sinning; second, to supply comfort and assurance to those who might sin, and, in consequence, be cast down and fearful that the issue would prove fatal. He, therefore, makes known to them the provision which God has made for just such an emergency. This we find at the end of verse 1 and throughout verse 2. The ground of comfort is twofold: let the downcast and repentant believer (1 Jn. 1:9) be assured that, first, he has an *"Advocate with the Father"*; second, that this Advocate is *"the propitiation for our sins"*. Now believers only may take comfort from this, for they alone have an *"Advocate"*, for them alone is Christ the propitiation, as is proven by linking the Propitiation ("and") with "the Advocate"!

In the second place, if other passages in the New Testament which speak of "propitiation," be compared with 1 John 2:2, it will be found that it is strictly limited in its scope. For example, in Romans 3:25 we read that God set forth Christ *"a propitiation through faith in His blood"*. If Christ is a propitiation "through faith", then he is not a "propitiation" to those who have no faith! Again, in Hebrews 2;17 we read, *"To make propitiation for the sins of the people"* (Heb. 2:17, R.V.).

In the third place, who are meant when John says, *"He is the propitiation for our sins"*? We answer, Jewish believers. And a part of the proof on which we base this assertion we now submit to the careful attention of the reader.

In Galatians 2:9 we are told that John, together with James and Cephas, were apostles *"unto the circumcision"* (i.e. Israel). In keeping with this, the Epistle of James is addressed to *"the twelve tribes, which are scattered abroad"* (1:1). So, the first Epistle of Peter is addressed to *"the elect who are sojourners of the dispersion"* (1 Pet. 1:1, R.V.). And John is also writing to saved Israelites, but for saved Jews and saved Gentiles.

Some of the evidences that John is writing to saved Jews are as follows. (a) In the opening verse he says of Christ, *"Which we have seen with our eyes....and our hands have handled"*. How impossible it would have been for the apostle Paul to have commenced any of his epistles to Gentile saints with such language!

(b) *"Brethren, I write no knew commandment unto you, but an old commandment which ye had from the beginning"* (1 John 2:7). The *"beginning"* here referred to is the beginning of the public manifestation of Christ-in proof compare 1:1; 2:13, etc. Now these believers the apostle tells us, had the *"old commandment"* from the beginning. This was true of Jewish believers, but it was not true of Gentile believers.

(c) *"I write unto you fathers, because ye have known Him from the beginning"* (2:13). Here, again, it is evident that it is Jewish believers that are in view.

(d) *"Little children, it is the last time: and as ye have heard that Antichrist shall come, even now are there many antichrists; whereby we know that it is the last time. They went out from us, but they were not of us"* (2: 18,19).

These brethren to whom John wrote had *"heard"* from Christ Himself that Antichrist should come (see Matthew 24). The *"many antichrists"* whom John declares *"went out from us"* were all Jews, for during the first century none but a Jew posed as the Messiah. Therefore, when John says *"He is the propitiation for our sins"* he can only mean for the sins of Jewish believers. (It is true that many things in John's Epistle apply equally to believing Jews *and* believing Gentiles. Christ is the Advocate of the one, as much as of the other. The same may be said of many things in the Epistle of James which is also a *catholic*, or general epistle, though expressly addressed to the twelve tribes scattered abroad.)

In the fourth place, when John added, *"And not for ours only, but also for the whole world"*, he signified that Christ was the propitiation for the sins of Gentile believers too, for, as previously shown, *"the world"* is a term contrasted from Israel. This interpretation is unequivocably established be a careful comparison of 1 John 2:2 with John 11:51,52, which is a strictly parallel passage: *"And this spake he not of himself: but being high priest that year, he prophesied that Jesus should die for that nation; And not for that nation only, but that also he should gather together in one the children of God that were scattered abroad"*. Here Caiaphas, under inspiration, made known for whom Jesus should *"die"*. Notice now the correspondency of his prophecy with this declaration of John's: *"He is the propitiation for our* (believing Israelites) *sins." "He prophesied that Jesus should die for that nation." "And not for ours only."* - That is, Gentile believers scattered throughout the earth. *"He should gather together in one of the children of God that were scattered abroad."*

In the fifth place, the above interpretation is confirmed by the fact that no other is consistent or intelligible. If the *"whole world"* signifies the whole human race, then the first clause and the *"also"* in the second clause are absolutely meaningless. If Christ is the propitiation for every-body, it would be idle tautology to say, first, *"He is the propitiation for our sins and also for everybody"*. The could be no *"also"* if He is the propitiation for the entire human family. Had the apostle meant to affirm that Christ is a universal propitiation he had omitted the first clause of verse 2, and simply said, *"He is the propitiation for the sins of the whole world"*. Confirmatory of *"not for ours* (Jewish believers) *only, but also for the whole world"* - Gentile believers, too; compare John 10:16; 17:20.

In the sixth place, our definition of *"the whole world"* is in perfect accord with other passages in the New Testament. For example: *"Whereof ye heard before in the word of the truth of the Gospel; which is come unto you, as it is in all the world"* (Col. 1:5,6). Does *"all the world"* here mean, absolutely and unqualifiedly, all mankind? Had all the human family heard the Gospel? No; the apostle's obvious meaning is that, the Gospel, instead of being confined to the land of Judea, had gone abroad, without restraint, into Gentile lands. So in Romans 1:8: *"First, I thank my God through Jesus Christ for you all, that your faith is spoken of throughout the whole world"*. The apostle is here referring to the faith of these Roman saints being spoken of in a way of commendation. But certainly all mankind did not so speak of their faith! It was the whole world of believers that he was referring to! In revelation 12:9 we read of Satan *"which deceiveth the whole world"*. But again this expression cannot be understood as a universal one, for Matthew 24:24 tell us that Satan does not and cannot *"deceive"* God's elect. Here it is *"the whole world"* of unbelievers.

In the seventh place, to insist that *"the whole world"* in 1 John 2:2 signifies the entire human race is to undermine the very foundations of our faith. If Christ is the propitiation for those that are lost equally as much as for those that are saved, then what assurance have we that believers too may not be lost? If Christ is the propitiation for those now in hell, what guarantee have I that I may not end in hell? The blood-shedding of the Incarnate Son of God is the only thing which can keep any one out of hell, and if many for whom that precious blood made propitiation are now in the awful place of the damned, then may not that blood prove inefficacious for me! Away with such a God-dishonoring thought.

However men may quibble and wrest the Scriptures, one thing is certain: The Atonement is no failure. God will not allow that precious and costly sacrifice to fail in accomplishing, completely, that which it was designed to effect. Not a drop of that holy blood was shed in vain. In the last great Day there shall stand forth no disappointed and defeated Savior, but One Who *"shall see of the travail of His soul and be satisfied"* (Isa. 53:11). These are not our words, but the infallible assertion of Him who declares, *"My counsel shall stand, and I will do all My pleasure"* (Isa. 64:10). Upon the impregnable rock we take our stand. Let others rest on the sands of human speculation and twentieth-century theorizing if they wish. That is their business. But to God they will yet have to render an account. For our part we had rather be railed at as a narrow-minded, out-of-date (people), than be found repudiating God's Truth by reducing the Divinely-efficacious atonement to a mere fiction.

Made in the USA
Monee, IL
03 May 2026

49437968R00036